Maxims of
La Rochefoucauld

• • •

ILLUSTRATED BY JAMES SCHWERING

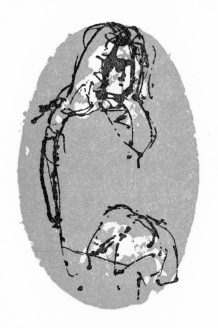

PETER PAUPER PRESS

MOUNT VERNON • NEW YORK

❡ NOTE

François de Marsillac, duc de la Rochefoucauld, was born in 1613 and died in 1680. A scion of one of the noblest families in France, he lived most of his life at the Court. There at a tender age he intrigued against Richelieu at the persuasion of Mme. de Chevreuse; later he intrigued against Mazarin at the persuasion of Mme. de Longueville. Still later, reduced to the status of a mere courtier, he was attached to Mme. de la Fayette, and he appears as the duc de Nemours in her historical novel La Princesse de Clèves. *But Rochefoucauld was more than a mere hand-kisser and intriguer. He merited the friendship of Mme. de Sévigné; and his* Reflexions, Sentences, et Maximes Morales, *first published in 1665, enjoyed the surprising popularity of five editions in his own lifetime. The present edition of this rather cynical book, which finds the source of all actions, good or bad, in self-interest, is in the translation specially made for the Peter Pauper Press in 1938. The present text contains most, but not all, of the original edition.*

OLD MEN love to give good advice; it consoles them for being able no longer to set a bad example.

• • •

Our passions are so surely governed by injustice and self-interest that they are dangerous guides; particularly suspect them when they appear most logical.

Explore as we may in the vast regions of self-esteem, undiscovered territories remain there still.

• • •

We think we are leading when we are being led: our minds seek one goal, while our hearts draw us all unknowing to another.

• • •

What we call virtue often is but a collection of casual actions and selfish interests which chance, or our own industry, manages to arrange. It is not always from valor that men are brave, nor from virtue that women are chaste.

• • •

Men would make us believe that the great and dazzling acts of history are the results of carefully thought-out plans; actually they are more often the results of men's moods and passions. Thus the war between Augustus and Anthony, ascribed to the desire of each to be the ruler of the world, was, perhaps, nothing but the result of personal jealousies.

• • •

Enthusiasm is the most convincing orator; it is like the functioning of an infallible law of nature. The simplest man, fired with enthusiasm, is more persuasive than the most eloquent without it.

In the human heart each generation of passions is succeeded by another; in the age of one arises the youth of the next.

. . .

Passions often produce their contraries: miserliness gives birth to generosity and generosity to miserliness; often we are bold through weakness, brave through timidity.

. . .

People are often vain of their most criminal passions; but envy is one passion so mean and low that nobody will admit to it.

. . .

Conceit endures less kindly censure of our taste than of our judgment.

. . .

Men are prone to forget benefits and injuries; they even learn to hate those who have helped them, and to forget those who have hurt them. The duty of gratitude or revenge is a slavery to which they will not submit.

. . .

The generosity of princes is often only policy: to buy the friendship of their people.

. . .

We all have strength to bear the misfortunes of our neighbors.

Self-control comes from man's fear of arousing jealousy and scorn in others by an ill-concealed elation over good fortune. Such strength of mind is but another vanity: exercised by great men to seem superior even to their acknowledged greatness.

. . .

Men condemned to die sometimes affect a fortitude and scorn of death that really is a fear of coming face to face with it; such fortitude and scorn are to the mind what a bandage is to the eyes.

. . .

Great men who finally break down under misfortunes give proof that till then they have been supported by ambitions and not by brains. Aside from a vast vanity, heroes are but ordinary men.

. . .

We do not open our hearts completely to our friends: not from distrust of them but from distrust of ourselves.

. . .

Conceal our passions as we may under the long cloaks of piety and of honor, still will the cloven hoof peep out.

. . .

Had we ourselves no faults we should find less pleasure discovering them in others.

Our pride rather than our virtue criticizes the faults of others: We reprove our friends less to correct their faults than to show that we ourselves are free of them.

•   •   •

It takes a better man to survive good luck than bad.

•   •   •

We can no more control the life of our passions than the length of our days.

Jealousy in a way is right and reasonable, for it defends what is ours, or what we think is ours; but envy cannot endure the happiness of others.

*   *   *

Jealousy thrives on doubt; certainty drives it to fury, or ends it altogether.

*   *   *

Pride is its own support; it loses nothing when vanity is cast away.

*   *   *

We promise according to our hopes, and perform according to our fears.

*   *   *

Self-interest speaks all tongues and plays all roles; even that of disinterest.

*   *   *

Self-interest blinds some men, and makes others see the light.

*   *   *

No accident so grave but that the clever man can turn it to some good; no luck so great but that the fool can twist it to his hurt.

*   *   *

Ancient philosophers' love of life or scorn of life was a matter of personal taste; no more to be reasoned with than our taste in foods or colors.

The philosophers' contempt of riches was only a concealed desire to avenge their merit against Fortune, by demeaning these blessings which Fortune had denied them. It was a stratagem to guard them against the degradations of poverty; it was a rule to gain the distinction they could not expect from wealth.

. . .

The hate of favorites is but the love of favor. We belittle those who enjoy it to salve our vanity at not enjoying it ourselves. We deny them our applause because we cannot deny the merit that brings them the applause of others.

. . .

To establish their position in the world, men go to any length to appear established already.

. . .

Some people are so self-centered that even in love they manage to be preoccupied with their own passion to the exclusion of their beloved.

. . .

Man's joy or sorrow depends as much upon his disposition as upon his fate.

. . .

Sincerity is an open heart. Few people show it; usually what we see is an imitation put on to snare the confidence of others.

11

A clever man should organize his self-interests in the order of their worth. Greediness often defeats its own ends, by making us scratch for every trifle when we should dig for gold alone.

. . .

What grace is to the body, reason is to the mind.

. . .

No disguise can long hide love where it exists, or feign it where it is not.

. . .

Since man does not command his love, no lover should demand constancy of his mistress, nor should she of him.

. . .

If we judge love by its results, it is more like hatred than affection.

. . .

It is easier to find a woman who has not sinned at all, than a woman who has sinned but once.

. . .

There is but one Love, yet his shape is legion.

. . .

True love is like a ghost: everyone talks of it, but few have met it face to face.

. . .

To be deceived by your friends is no disgrace; to distrust them is.

Love lends its name to many transactions in which it has no more part than the Doge has in the infinite doings of Venice.

* * *

Virtue serves our selfish interests as well as vice.

We praise in others what we find in ourselves; true friendship grows when self-esteem is flattered by mutual agreement in tastes and pleasures.

* * *

We become reconciled with our enemies because we want to improve our situation, because we are weary of war, or because we fear defeat.

* * *

What men call friendship is but a partnership for pooling interests and exchanging favors — a transaction in which self-esteem always expects to profit.

* * *

Self-interest, and not love, urges our friendship for those in power; we give our hearts away that we, not they, may profit.

* * *

The grandest ambition looks least like it when faced with the impossible.

* * *

Our self-esteem judges the worth of others by the pleasure their friendship gives us; we measure their merit by their treatment of us.

* * *

A great name degrades rather than exalts those unworthy to bear it.

Our strength exceeds our will; how often we say things are impossible when we are looking for an excuse.

. . .

In our relations with men we please more by our faults than by our virtues.

. . .

The greatest proof of merit is to hear it praised even by the most envious.

. . .

The head is ever the dupe of the heart.

. . .

Men and their actions must be seen in proper perspective; some are judged best close at hand, some at a distance.

. . .

To stumble upon knowledge is not to be wise; the true sage understands, selects, and proves his wisdom.

. . .

One form of coquetry: to boast of never flirting.

. . .

Youth changes its tastes by force of passion; age retains its tastes by force of habit.

. . .

There are some whose faults do them honor; some whose virtues disgrace them.

Many marriages are good; none are pleasant.

. . .

The blemishes of the mind, like those of the face, increase with age.

. . .

We never forgive a betrayal by a friend or by a foe; yet often we are content to betray ourselves.

. . .

We work so consistently to disguise ourselves to others that we end by being disguised to ourselves.

. . .

Man is never less sincere than when he asks, or offers, advice. When he asks it he seems to defer to the wisdom of his friend, but really he seeks approval of his own opinion, and to make his friend responsible with him for his actions. When he offers advice, he seems to repay the confidence of his inquirer with disinterested zeal, while really seeking to bolster his own advantage or reputation.

. . .

Nothing is so liberally given as advice.

. . .

It is easier to deceive yourself, and to do so unperceived, than to deceive another.

Repentance is not so much sorrow for our misdeeds as fear of possible punishment.

• • •

The charm of novelty and the permanency of habit, opposite as they are, both blind us equally to the faults of our friends.

A light woman's smallest fault is her vice.

. . .

Habitual trickery marks a little mind. He who protects himself on one flank with deceit generally lays himself open to attack on another.

. . .

The only good imitation is that which shows the absurdity of a bad original.

. . .

We are never so ridiculous from the qualities we have as from those we affect.

. . .

We would rather speak ill of ourselves than not speak of ourselves at all.

. . .

The reason so few men can carry on a sensible and agreeable conversation is that hardly one but thinks more of what he himself intends to say than of what is being said to him by others. Sometimes even the cleverest and politest man only feigns attention, while we can see by his eyes that his mind has gone back to polish up his own remarks. He does not consider that the worst way to win over others is to talk for his own pleasure, and that the best conversationalist is he who listens with care and answers to the point.

Some there are who would never have been in love, had they never learned the word.

. . .

Deprived of the company of fools, a great wit does not seem half so clever.

. . .

We often boast that we are never boring to ourselves; our vanity prevents us from seeing how boring we can be to others.

. . .

As it is the mark of a great mind to say much in few words, so is it the mark of a little one to talk much and say little.

. . .

Often we exaggerate the goodness of others more for our own virtue in giving praise than for the virtues that we praise: thus we invite commendation by seeming to dispense it.

. . .

Flattery is base coin; only our vanity gives it currency.

. . .

Our wish to deserve the praise given us sharpens our merits; praise of our wisdom, our bravery or our beauty tends to increase them.

. . .

We disavow praise so as to be praised again.

More things are left undone through neglect of duty than through neglect of self-interest.

*   *   *

It is not enough to have great qualities; we must also have the management of them.

*   *   *

However brilliant an act, it may not be judged great unless resulting from a noble motive.

*   *   *

It is easier to seem fitted for posts we covet, than to carry out the duties of those we possess.

*   *   *

When a man's acts are honest and just, it is hard to know if they result from righteousness or cleverness.

*   *   *

Greed is more nearly the opposite of economy than of liberality.

*   *   *

Hope, though she often deceives us, still leads us pleasantly down the paths of life.

*   *   *

Though idleness and fear may keep us in the road of duty, virtue usually gets the praise.

*   *   *

The world oftener applauds the appearance of virtue than it does virtue itself.

We may say that vices lie before us like inns
along the road of life; even if we traveled the
same road over again, I doubt if experience
would teach us to avoid them.

We do not despise all who have vices; we do despise all who have no virtues.

. . .

Pride more often than ignorance makes us refuse to accept new ideas: finding the first places taken in the intellectual parade, we refuse to take the last.

. . .

Learn to bear the ills you have, before worrying how to bear the ones you fear may come.

. . .

Constancy in love is a perpetual inconstancy. We love in succession all the virtues of a mistress, dwelling now on one and now on another, until constancy becomes inconstancy within the limit of one person.

. . .

In love there are two kinds of constancy: in one we continue to find new virtues to love in the same mistress; in the other we remain constant as a point of honor.

. . .

Constancy deserves neither praise nor censure; it is but the continuance of feelings and desires whose nature we cannot control.

. . .

The highest skill is the true judgment of values.

When our vices abandon us we flatter ourselves
that we have abandoned them.

. . .

The man who never gives way to folly is not as
wise as he thinks.

. . .

Crime as well as virtue has its heroes.

. . .

What often keeps us from abandoning a single
particular vice is the weakness induced by
many.

. . .

We easily forget those faults that are known to
ourselves alone.

. . .

Of some men we cannot believe evil till we see
it; and yet in few does it come as a surprise.

. . .

Coldness in woman, like a gaud, is something
put on to increase the allure.

. . .

Virtue in women is often the love of a good
reputation or a peaceful conscience.

. . .

Folly follows us through life; we call that man
wise whose folly is in proportion to his age, and
to his wealth.

Perfect valor is to do without witnesses what you would do before the world.

· · ·

In battle most men expose themselves enough to satisfy the needs of honor; few wish to do more than this, or more than enough to carry to success the action in which they are engaged.

· · ·

Hypocrisy is the homage vice pays to virtue.

· · ·

Vanity, shame, and disposition above all, make men brave and women chaste.

· · ·

With the approach of old age few people fail to reveal their weaknesses of mind and body.

· · ·

Gratitude is like credit; it is the backbone of our social commerce. We pay our debts not so much because it is right to do so, as because we hope to gain credit again later in the same place.

· · ·

Conceit is more cunning even than the most subtle courtier.

· · ·

Passion often makes fools of clever men; sometimes even makes clever men of fools.

People who merely pay the debts of gratitude cannot flatter themselves they are truly grateful.

. . .

The gratitude we expect and the gratitude we receive never jibe; for the pride of the giver and the pride of the receiver never agree on the value of a service rendered.

. . .

Too great a zeal in discharging an obligation is a kind of ingratitude.

. . .

To accept present favors from a man makes us swallow the injuries he has dealt us in the past.

. . .

Usually we give praise only to beget it.

. . .

Nothing is so infectious as example; and our noblest and most vicious acts reproduce themselves. Imitation of a noble act is emulation; imitation of a vicious act is release of our evil nature through the force of example.

. . .

It is great folly to wish only to be wise.

. . .

We are easily consoled at the misfortunes of a friend when they enable us to exhibit our sympathy for him.

Sorrow is riddled with many hypocrisies. Thus when we mourn a friend, it is for ourselves that we grieve; for the loss of our friend's respect, or our comfort, or pleasures, or monetary reward. In this way the dead get credit for tears bestowed upon the living. Such tears I term hypocrisy, for in them we deceive ourselves. Another sort of hypocrisy is less innocent than this, for it deceives the world: this is the grief of those who aspire to an immortal sorrow. After time, which heals all wounds, has absorbed what sorrow they may have had, they still obstinately shower their tears, their sighs and their groans upon all men; they put on a grief-stricken mien, and by their actions would make you think their sorrow will end only with the grave. This unpleasant and distressing vanity is commonly found in ambitious women. Barred by their sex from the usual roads to glory, they seek fame by exhibiting an unconsolable grief. There is still a third sort of hypocrisy, that of tears which flow from little wells: these spill and cease with equal facility. Such hypocrites weep to gain a reputation for tenderness; weep to be pitied; weep to be bewept in turn; — weep even so as not to be seen unweeping.

* * *

Every one blames his memory; no one blames his judgment.

No one should be praised for goodness who has not strength for wickedness. Most goodness is but laziness or lack of will.

. . .

What seems to be generosity sometimes is ambition, which throws away trifles in its search for bigger game.

. . .

In most men loyalty is a device of self-interest; a means of exalting themselves, and of becoming the depositaries of valuable trusts.

. . .

Vices enter into the composition of virtues as poisons into medicines; wisdom collects and blends them to offset the ills of life.

. . .

It is as common to change one's tastes as it is uncommon to change one's character.

. . .

Humility is often a feigned submission whose object is to make others submit to us. It is a trick whereby pride lowers itself in a thousand ways, but it is never so well disguised or so apt at deceit as when cloaked in seeming humility.

. . .

Gravity is an imposing carriage of the body designed to conceal the absence of the mind.

We deceive ourselves if we believe that among passions the violent ones like love and ambition are masters over the others. Idleness, unaggressive as she is, is the real sovereign; she usurps authority over all the plans and actions of our lives, little by little swallowing passions and virtues alike.

.   .   .

The pleasure of love is in loving; we are happier in the passion we feel than in the passion we inspire.

.   .   .

Pity is often a realization of our own troubles through the troubles of others: a subtle preparation for our own evil days. We help others so that under similar circumstances they will help us, and the service we render them is in reality a service to ourselves in anticipation.

.   .   .

A narrow mind begets obstinacy; it is hard to be persuaded of something beyond the scope of our understanding.

.   .   .

No man is clever enough to realize to the full all the evil he does.

.   .   .

Pride, which inspires envy, can smother it too.

What we call liberality is often the vanity of giving — a thing we like more than the thing we give away.

. . .

Often we forego love for ambition; never ambition for love.

Some lies are so well disguised to resemble truth, that we should be poor judges of the truth not to believe them.

.   .   .

Novelty is to love as the flower is to the fruit: it lends a glamor which is quickly lost, never to return.

.   .   .

Some disgust us with their virtues; others attract us even in their faults.

.   .   .

Absence extinguishes small passions and increases great ones, just as a wind will snuff a candle or fan a fire.

.   .   .

Many a woman thinks herself in love when she is not; the excitement of intrigue, the amorous reaction to gallantry, the natural wish to be loved, and the difficulty of saying no, combine to persuade her that she has passion when she has only coquetry.

.   .   .

We give praise to struggling newcomers from envy of those who are firmly established.

.   .   .

We must admit to the credit of virtue that man's greatest woes come from his crimes.

Readiness to believe evil, without examining the facts, is an effect of pride and laziness. We are quick to proclaim our discovery of criminals; but we are slow to inquire into their crimes.

. . .

Moderation has been made a virtue so as to curb the ambition of the great, and console the ordinary for their small fortunes and small deserts.

. . .

It is impossible to love a second time someone whom we have really ceased to love.

. . .

We always find several solutions to the same problem: not from resourcefulness of mind, but from obtuseness, which stops at every possibility, and so prevents our choosing the best solution at once.

. . .

Some troubles, like some sicknesses, are made worse by attempted cures; the greatest skill is to know when to keep from interfering with Nature.

. . .

Vanity is the greatest of all flatterers.

. . .

We always like our admirers; we do not always like those we admire.

Sometimes it takes greater wisdom to follow good advice than to give it.

· · ·

Some evil folk would be much less dangerous if they had not a few virtues too.

· · ·

Nearly everyone is pleased to acknowledge a small indebtedness; many are grateful in acknowledging a moderate one; but there is hardly a man who does not, for a really great indebtedness, return ingratitude.

· · ·

Usually only in trifles are we bold enough not to trust appearances.

· · ·

We forgive people who bore us; never those we bore.

· · ·

Self-interest, blamed for all our ill deeds, should often be praised for our good ones.

· · ·

It is as right to boast to ourselves as it is wrong to do so to the world.

· · ·

Some people are fated to be fools; they commit follies not only of their own will, but because they are predestined to do so.

At times, when we are working to help others,
self-interest seems to be the dupe of good-will;
and yet there is no surer path to our own bene-
fit, for we are extending usury under the guise

of charity, and in a subtle and pleasing manner gaining general esteem for ourselves.

* * *

Some follies are as catching as disease.

* * *

If some men do not appear to be fools, it is only that their folly has not yet been deeply searched for.

* * *

Lovers never tire of each other: they speak always of themselves.

* * *

How is it that our memory is good enough to remember the slightest triviality in our lives, but not good enough to remember how often we have told it to the same person.

* * *

The extreme delight we take in talking about ourselves should make us suspect that it is not shared by those who listen.

* * *

To praise princes for virtues they do not possess is a way to insult them with impunity.

* * *

We are more apt to love those who hate us, than those who love us too much.

Ridicule dishonors us more than disgrace itself.

. . .

We admit to small faults that our claims to have no large ones may bear weight.

. . .

Envy is more implacable than hate.

. . .

Sometimes we think we dislike flattery: we dislike only the method.

. . .

It is harder to be faithful to a mistress when she is devoted than when she is evil-tempered.

. . .

Women are less the slaves of their passions than their coquetries.

. . .

We have certain good qualities that are like the five senses: those who lack them can neither see nor understand them.

. . .

We are conscious of our good or evil fortune in proportion to our vanity.

. . .

The cleverness of most women serves their folly rather than their wisdom.

Our native accent lives in our hearts and minds, as well as in our tongues.

. . .

Some bad qualities make great talents.

. . .

Little minds are easily wounded by little things; great minds experience all things, and even so are left unscathed.

. . .

We seldom judge a man to be sensible unless his ideas agree with ours.

. . .

Lovers are prompt to forget all the truths they have taken years to learn.

. . .

Love's greatest miracle: the exorcisement of coquetry in women.

. . .

Those who deceive us we hate with a special bitterness, for they think themselves cleverer than we are.

. . .

A gentleman may love like a lunatic, but not like a beast.

. . .

We are always bored by those great ones with whom it is not permitted to be bored.

Opportunities make us known to others; even more to ourselves.

• • •

It is particularly hard to break off an affair, when the love that began it is dead.

• • •

We all know that it is bad taste to talk about our wives; not all of us realize that it is worse to talk about ourselves.

• • •

When we lose friends sometimes our grief is greater than our mourning, sometimes our mourning greater than our grief.

• • •

The smallest infidelity to ourselves humiliates us more than our greatest to others.

• • •

Jealousy and love are always born together; usually they die apart.

• • •

Most women grieve for the death of a lover, not so much for love's sake as to show that they are worthy to be loved.

• • •

The evils we inflict on others give us less pain than those we inflict on ourselves.

There are certain vices which, when they are well mounted, glitter like the jewel virtue itself.

. . .

Usually we praise heartily only those who admire us.

. . .

However we may distrust the sincerity of those we talk with, we always believe they are more sincere with us than with others.

. . .

There are but few virtuous women who are not weary of the part.

. . .

Most chaste women are like hidden treasures: safe, because no one is searching for them.

. . .

The commonest trouble with a mistress is: she can't see that love is dead.

. . .

The subtlest deception is to feign stepping into snares we know are laid for us. Men are never so easily deceived as when trying to deceive others.

. . .

What we call our sincerity is mostly the desire to talk about ourselves, and to put our faults in the best possible light.

If vanity does not overthrow all our virtues, at least she makes them totter.

. . .

What makes the vanity of others insupportable is that it wounds our own.

. . .

Fortune seems most blind to those on whom she has never turned her face.

. . .

When other men are caught in our snares we do not think them so foolish: but how ridiculously foolish we seem to ourselves when caught in the snares of others!

. . .

Though we are not bold enough to say we have no faults and our enemies have no virtues, still we are not far from thinking so.

. . .

There is a kind of greatness that does not depend on wealth. It is a certain air of distinction that seems to destine us for great things; a high valuation we unconsciously set upon ourselves, whereby we gain the deference of others, and, more than by birth, wealth, or even merit itself, are raised to greatness.

. . .

True wisdom gets angry at nothing.

We are less unhappy to be deceived by one we love, than to be undeceived by her.

. . .

We keep our first lover a long time — if we do not get a second.

. . .

What there is least of in gallantry is love.

. . .

Nature seems to have hidden a certain genius so deep within us that we are unaware of its existence until passion brings it out, giving us a wisdom and power that art, or education, could never teach us.

. . .

Each age of life is new to us; no matter how old we are we still are troubled by inexperience.

. . .

Every passion leads us into some faults; love alone makes us ridiculous.

. . .

Few people know how to act old.

. . .

The most dangerous folly of old people who once were gay and charming, is to forget they are no longer so.

. . .

If people could see our motives, we should often be ashamed of our noblest actions.

40

In all walks of life people assume the role, the gestures, and the costume they wish the world to see. Thus we live in a world of actors.

* * *

Weakness, not vice, is the enemy of virtue.

41

The coquette makes a point of being jealous of her lovers: thus she masks her jealousy of other women.

. . .

Wit sometimes enables us to be rude with impunity.

. . .

The vivacity which increases with old age is not far removed from folly.

. . .

It takes friends to sicken us of friendship, worshippers to sicken us of piety.

. . .

It is easy to forgive in our friends those vices they do not inflict upon us.

. . .

In the old age of love, just as in the old age of life, we find we have survived for discomforts, not for joys.

. . .

We credit ourselves with the vices we do not have: thus if we are weak, we boast of our obstinacy.

. . .

Penetration of mind has a spice of prophecy in it which flatters our vanity more than any other quality of the intellect.

Young women who do not want to seem co-
quettes, and old men who do not want to seem
ridiculous, should not talk of love and of themselves in the same breath.

. . .

We often think we bear misfortunes with dig-
nity, whereas really we are too stunned to move;
we suffer without daring to look our troubles
in the eye, like a coward killed because he is
afraid to defend himself.

. . .

Women in love will more readily forgive a great
infidelity than a little indiscretion.

. . .

After people have deceived us, we owe them
nothing beyond indifference in their friendship;
but we always owe them sympathy in their
sorrows.

. . .

Women are little given to friendship, for it is
insipid after love.

. . .

In love, as in friendship, we are happier through
ignorance than knowledge.

. . .

We make a virtue of the vices we do not want
to correct.

Shame and jealousy are so painful because our vanity cannot salve them.

.   .   .

Propriety is the least of laws, but the best observed.

.   .   .

Our pride is greatly increased by each little fault we forego.

.   .   .

No one believes himself inferior in every respect to the man he considers the ablest among his friends.

.   .   .

Sometimes we meet a fool with wit; never with discretion.

.   .   .

Our enemies come nearer the truth when they judge us than when we judge ourselves.

.   .   .

There are various remedies for the cure of love, none infallible.

.   .   .

Age is a tyrant that forbids, under pain of death, the enjoyment of the pleasures of youth.

.   .   .

The same pride that makes us condemn the vices from which we think ourselves free, makes us belittle the virtues we know we lack.

44

We should gain more in the end by letting the world see what we are, than by trying to seem what we are not.

• • •

There are two kinds of curiosity: one arises from self-interest, that wishes to learn everything that may be to our advantage, and the other from vanity, that wishes to know more than our neighbors.

Nothing should so humiliate men who have received great praise, as their acquiring it through the smallest means.

. . .

We should judge a man not by his abilities, but by his use of them.

. . .

In their first passion women love their lovers; in later passions they love love.

. . .

Pride, like other passions, has its follies. We are ashamed to admit to present jealousy, although we boast of our great jealousy in the past, and threaten to exhibit it again.

. . .

Nothing is rarer than true good-nature. Those who think they have it are usually only easy-going, or weak.

. . .

The same strength of character that enables us to resist love, makes love more enduring and strong when we come to it. Weak natures that are always succumbing to passion rarely feel it very deeply, or for long.

. . .

We confide our deepest secrets to our friends so that they can pity or envy us.

46

Love of glory, fear of shame, desire for a life of ease and comfort, greed for reward, or wish to lord it over our neighbors: these cause the bravery we are so proud of.

. . .

There is no praise we have not lavished upon Prudence; but where is the smallest success she can promise us?

. . .

Man's hatred of lies often is an unconscious ambition to give weight to his own words, which he would have carry the sanctity of truth.

. . .

However wicked men may be, they do not dare to condemn virtue openly; thus when they wish to damage virtue they pretend it is false, or charge it with crimes.

. . .

Young men entering life should seem either shy or bold; for poise and self-possession in those so young soon turn into impertinence.

. . .

Extreme avarice almost always defeats itself. No passion more often fails of its object, and in none does present self-interest wield such compelling power to the prejudice of the future.

47

Whatever difference may appear in men's fortunes, there is always a certain balance of joy and sorrow which makes them equal.

* * *

What makes it clear that men know their faults better than we suspect is that they never admit to them in describing their own conduct. Thus conceit, that usually blinds men, enlightens them then, and puts them on guard to disguise or censor the smallest fault.

* * *

We pay no attention to a woman's first affair until she indulges in her second.

* * *

A small mind with good-nature bores less in the long run than a great mind with an evil nature.

* * *

Jealousy is the worst of our ills; but it is the least pitied by those who cause it.

* * *

We seldom strike a bad bargain by foregoing the good things people say of us in return for their promise to say no evil.

* * *

Self-satisfied men persuade themselves to be proud of their misfortunes; thus they seek to persuade others that they alone are worthy of the shafts of fate.

No one wishes to lose his life, while everyone wishes to win glory; this is why brave men show even more caution and skill in preserving their lives than usurers do in preserving their fortunes.

• • •

The mind is as susceptible to infection as the body; no matter how secure we consider ourselves from passion, our minds still are as subject to it as our bodies are to disease.

• • •

When reason cannot console us for our little evils, we sometimes comfort ourselves that they are not great ones.

• • •

Often we conceal venom in the arrow of our praise, to poison reputation in the guise of pointing to it.

• • •

A beneficiary is often ungrateful; but generally less so than his benefactor.

• • •

We are mistaken if we distinguish between mind and judgment: judgment is but the light of the mind. Judgment goes to the root of matters, it illumines all that is obvious, and makes visible what is hidden. Thus to the lantern of the mind, that enables us to see deep into the heart of things, should go the credit which we give to judgment.

50

Knowledge lies in the understanding of details; and since the number of details is infinite, ours will always be a superficial and an imperfect knowledge.

. . .

Often we are treacherous more from weariness than from intent to deceive.

. . .

Frequently we do good so that later we may do evil with impunity.

. . .

The subtlest contrivers spend their days in decrying deceit, so that they can employ it unsuspected in a time of crucial need.

. . .

Sometimes we must play the fool to escape the wiles of a clever deceiver.

. . .

The prosperous are peaceful: good fortune soothes the temper.

. . .

Philosophy is lord of past and future ills; the slave of present ones.

. . .

Pride is much the same in all men; but they differ in the ways they show it.

Like farces, the repute of some people is short-lived.

. . .

Few things are impossible in themselves; diligence in carrying it out fails us more often than the method employed.

. . .

Youth is a continual intoxication; it is a delirium of the reason.

. . .

We exaggerate the affection of our friends less in gratitude to them than in exaltation of ourselves.

. . .

When men enumerate our virtues they tell us nothing new.

. . .

One kind of love is so excessive there is no room for jealousy.

. . .

Of all our faults we most readily admit that of idleness. We make ourselves believe it is a philosophical virtue in itself; and that instead of destroying all other virtues, it merely suspends their functioning.

. . .

We find few ungrateful people when we are able to bestow favors.

The restraints we put upon ourselves to keep from falling in love often hurt more than the pangs of unrequited love itself.

. . .

We are equally unhappy when we are deeply in love, and when we have no lover at all.

. . .

It is a small misfortune to oblige an ingrate; it is a great misfortune to be indebted to a scoundrel.

. . .

The passion to seem clever often keeps us from being so.

. . .

Virtue would not go so far, did not Vanity escort her.

. . .

Man apparently finds himself insufficiently supplied with faults; for he increases them with various strange habits, which he affects and cultivates so assiduously that at length they become natural to him and no longer to be corrected.

. . .

Our envy always outlasts the happiness we are envying.

. . .

Those who have experienced the pain of a great passion bewail their cure the rest of their days.

If we conquer our passions it is more through their weakness than our strength.

.   .   .

We admit our faults so that our sincerity may repair our damaged reputations.

.   .   .

In most men the love of justice to all is but the fear of injustice to themselves.

.   .   .

He who thinks he has power to satisfy the world, deceives himself; but he who thinks the world can not be satisfied with him, deceives himself still more.

.   .   .

False sincerity disguises its faults both to itself and others; true sincerity knows its faults perfectly and confesses them.

.   .   .

That man is truly good and honest who invites the scrutiny of good and honest men.

.   .   .

Some fools know their weakness, and use it to their gain.

.   .   .

With age we become more foolish — and more wise.

54

The stresses of fortune, like a lamp, bring out our vices and virtues into bold relief.

.   .   .

Persecution and hate pursue our bad qualities less than our good.

.   .   .

We satirize from vanity, not from malice.

.   .   .

It seems that nature, that has wisely ordered our bodies for our happiness, gave us pride too, to spare us the mortification of knowing our shortcomings.

.   .   .

Flatter ourselves as we may with our great achievements, Fortune is more responsible than forethought.

.   .   .

Our actions are governed by good and evil stars; to them we owe the blame or praise that is our lot.

.   .   .

Great as are the advantages given by Nature, it takes the aid of Fortune too to make the hero.

.   .   .

For him who does not trust himself, silence is the best defense.

The mind's politeness: delicacy and purity of thought.

. . .

The mind's gallantry: pleasing and tactful statement.

. . .

Truth works less good in this world than its counterfeits work evil.

. . .

Our faults are generally more excusable than the means we take to hide them.

. . .

We do not like to give praise, and do not do so without some self-centered motive. Praise is a subtle dissembling flattery, pleasing him who praises as well as him who is praised: the one accepts it as a reward of merit, the other extends it as a sign of his own justice and good judgment.

. . .

We enter new studies not so much from weariness of the old, or desire for change, as from a desire to be admired by those who are wiser than we, and a hope of gaining advantage over those who are not.

. . .

We often complain lightly of our friends: thus we justify in advance our own similar failings.

Death and the sun are two things no man can
outstare.

• • •

Honors are to merit what dress is to a pretty
woman.

57

One sort of vacillation comes from the lightness and weakness of intellect that make us accept every opinion as we hear it; a more excusable sort results from a surfeit of arguments.

.   .   .

A nature which is boastful of its generosity often withdraws it at the slightest call of self-interest.

.   .   .

The gratitude of most men is but a secret desire to encourage further benefits.

.   .   .

Innocence is lucky if it finds the same protection as guilt.

.   .   .

We should manage fortune like our health: enjoy it when it is good, be patient when it is bad, and resort to heroic remedies only in extremity.

.   .   .

Magnanimity defines itself; but we can add that it is the good common-sense of pride, the noblest road to praise.

.   .   .

When we heartily praise good deeds, we seem to share in the credit for them.

❲ ON THE SCORN OF DEATH

Having treated of the hollowness of so many seeming virtues, it is appropriate now to treat of the hollowness of our scorn of death. I mean that scorn of death which pagans boast of as coming from their own courage, without any hope of a future life. There is a difference between meeting death with a brave face, and in belittling it: the first is common enough, but the second, I fear, is nothing but bravado.

Everything has been written that could be written to prove that death is no misfortune; and the weakest of men, as well as the bravest, have given innumerable proofs that this should be true; and yet I do not believe any sensible person ever believed it. The very pains we take to persuade ourselves, as well as others, that it is true, show well enough how hard it is to be convincing on that subject.

For many reasons we may be disgusted with life, but for none may we despise its curtain: for even those who would take their own lives cannot think lightly of the matter, and are as startled, and struggle as fiercely as anyone, if death comes for them in a guise they have not themselves selected. And the differences we see in brave men's bravery is just this: that they suddenly see death closer to them at one time than another, or see it in an unexpected guise. Thus it comes about that having despised what they were in ignorance of, they learn to fear what they have come to see and know.

The wisest and most sensible are those who take the best means to avoid reflecting on death, for every man who sees it in its true light knows that it is the worst of all calamities. The inevitability of death caused all the stoicism of the philosophers: they thought it but right to go with a good grace when they must go, and being unable to perpetuate their lives, they labored to perpetuate their words and reputations, thus to save from the wreck all that might be saved.

To put a good face on the matter, let us be content not to admit to ourselves all that we think of death, but to trust to our good dispositions to help us, rather than our fallible reasoning, which tries to build up our indifference. The glory of a courageous death, the hope of being regretted, the desire to leave a good name behind us, the assurance of being freed of the miseries of life, and of being independent of the whims of fortune, these are all things we must remember. But as antidotes for the pain of death they are far from infallible. They give us the same kind of assurance a hedge gives to soldiers storming a fortress. It looks like shelter from a distance, but at close range it gives but little protection, serving best as a screen between our eyes and doom. We only deceive ourselves to think that death at arm's length will look the same as from afar, and that our feelings, which are but weaknesses, are strong enough to withstand the fiercest of all trials. We are equally absurd to count on our pride to face down an ordeal which it knows will destroy it.

And as for our powers of reasoning, they too will be too weak to persuade us that all is well. Our common-sense, indeed, instead of teaching us to scorn death, makes us all too aware of its terrors. The best that common-sense can do for us is persuade us to look the other way, at less fearful things. Cato and Brutus chose noble things; a lackey not long since contented himself with dancing on the scaffold where he was about to die.

Thus, however diverse the motives, they all come to the same end. Indeed, whatever the difference between the noble and the peasant, we have often seen each of them meet death with the same calm, but always with this distinction: the indifference of the noble comes from thoughts of glory, which screen him from the sight of death; while the indifference of the peasant comes from his limited understanding, which hides from him the horror of his calamity, and leaves him free to think of other things.